THREE JEWISH PLAYS

by
DAVID MAMET

SAMUEL FRENCH, INC.
45 WEST 25TH STREET NEW YORK 10010
7623 SUNSET BOULEVARD HOLLYWOOD 90046
LONDON TORONTO

ISBN 0 573 69066 9 Printed in U.S.A.

THE DISAPPEARANCE OF THE JEWS

THE CHARACTERS

BOBBY............................*in his late thirties*

JOEY..............................*in his late thirties*

THE SCENE

A hotel room, Chicago

THE DISAPPEARANCE OF THE JEWS was first presented at the Goodman Theatre in Chicago. The production was directed by Gregory Mosher. The cast was:

BOBBY .... Norman Parker
JOEY................................ Joe Mantegna

THE DISAPPEARANCE OF THE JEWS

SCENE ONE

JOEY. What *I* remember ... what I remember was that time we were at Ka-Ga-Wak we took Howie Greenberg outside.

BOBBY. Was that Howie Greenberg?

JOEY. Yeah...

BOBBY. No...

JOEY. No? Who was it, then?

BOBBY. *(pause)* It...

JOEY. It was Howie Greenberg.

BOBBY. RED hair...

JOEY. Yeah. Red hair. Braces.

BOBBY. *(pause)* That was Howie Greenberg?

JOEY. Yeah.

BOBBY. From Rodfei Zedek?

JOEY. No. He never went to Rodfei?

BOBBY. No?

JOEY. No. Hey, Bob, no, *you* never went to Rodfei.

BOBBY. What's that mean, I don't know who *went* there...?

JOEY. *(pause)* No. It doesn't mean that. But you know the time I'm talking of?

BOBBY. We tied him to the bed. We put him in the snow.

JOEY. Yeah.

BOBBY. I got to tell you something, Joey, it was *not* Howie Greenberg. *Howie* never went to Winter Camp. *(pause)* Am I right? *(pause)* Am I right?
Jeff went to Winter Camp. Tell me I'm wrong. *(pause)* You fuckin' asshole...

JOEY. *You, you,* what the fuck would *you* know, never even get a Christmas card from you: "What happened to who." It was *Jeff*...?

BOBBY. Yeah. *(pause)*

JOEY. Isn't that funny...I'm not sure you're right... *(pause)* Huh...

BOBBY. Whatever happened to Howie?

JOEY. *Howie.*

BOBBY. Yeah.

JOEY. Are you ready for this...? Howie turned out to be a fag.

BOBBY. You're kidding.

JOEY. No.

BOBBY. You're kidding.

JOEY. No.

BOBBY. How about that.

JOEY. Isn't that something.

BOBBY. Yeah. *(pause)* His parents?

JOEY. Moved to Florida. *(pause)*

BOBBY. I always liked him.

JOEY. I did, too. *(pause)*

BOBBY. Huh. *(pause)*

JOEY. Yeah.

BOBBY. What ever happened to *Jeff?*

JOEY. He's still here...

SCENE TWO

JOEY. I was thinking I was up on *Devon* ... *You 'member when we used to take the Ravenswood...?*

BOBBY. When? See the *Cubs...?*

JOEY. Yeah.

BOBBY. *Oh* yeah ... Is that joint still there?

JOEY. What? *Frankels...?*

BOBBY. On *Devon...?*

JOEY. The *Roastbeef...?*

BOBBY. Yeah.

JOEY. Yeah. It's still there. It isn't on Devon.

BOBBY. No?

JOEY. It's on Petersen. It's in Rogers *Park. (pause)*

BOBBY. You 'member those two broads we had?

JOEY. The Rogers Park broads?

BOBBY. The *folk*dancing broads...

JOEY. ...yeah...

BOBBY. The two *Debbies...*

JOEY. Debbie. Yeah. Right.

BOBBY. Rubovitz and Rosen.

JOEY. Debbie Rubovitz and Rosen.

BOBBY. For five bucks which one was mine?

JOEY. I don't know.

BOBBY. For ten bucks?

JOEY. Rosen.

BOBBY. You're full of shit.

JOEY. Rosen. You owe me ten bucks.

BOBBY. It wasn't Rosen.

JOEY. *You* don't know, you *fuck,* you're *bull*shitting me. You don't remember.

BOBBY. I remember. Mine was Rosen.

JOEY. That's what I said.

BOBBY. No.

JOEY. You said "Which one was Rosen." I said *yours.*

BOBBY. She *was...? (pause)*

JOEY. *I* don't remember...

BOBBY. Which was the *short* one...?

JOEY. Yours. Right? With the curly hair...?

BOBBY. And which one was her name?

JOEY. I don't know. *(pause)*

BOBBY. Whatever you think happened to those broads?

JOEY. I don't know.

BOBBY. You ever think about them?

JOEY. Very seldom. When I go through Rogers Park. *(pause)*

BOBBY. You think they were dykes?

JOEY. I don't *know.* D'you think that?

BOBBY. I kind of did.

JOEY. I kind of did, too.

BOBBY. At the time?

JOEY. No. Are you *kidding* me...? Who knew? I tell you what I think: they were before their time.

BOBBY. *Oh* yeah...they were...

JOEY. They were before their time...I tell you how I always knew the broad was yours, the broad she couldn't find her way outta the *bathroom* that was yours...

BOBBY. And what were you, a *head* man...?

JOEY. Except for *Deenie,* of course. Yes, I was a head

man, yeah...

BOBBY. You wanted to discuss, *what...?*

JOEY. ...the broad, she couldn't find the *light* switch, that was yours...

BOBBY. ...some intellectual giants...

JOEY. ...that's right...

BOBBY. "Tell us about Moby *Dick*"...

JOEY. You *wished...*

BOBBY. And so which broad was mine?

JOEY. *Rosen*...I don't know...*Rubovitz*...Rogers Park... what the hell...*(pause)* Some *Jew* broad...*(pause)* Some *folk dancer.* I don't know...the *short* one. *(pause)* Some broad... How's Laurie?

BOBBY. Fine.

JOEY. Yeah, but how *is* she, though...?

BOBBY. She's *fine.* What did I *say?*

JOEY. You said that she was *fine. (pause)*

BOBBY. *Alright. (pause)*

JOEY. *So? (pause)*

BOBBY. So *what?*

JOEY. Yeah. So *what,* so how *is* she, you give me this *shit* all the time...you never fuckin' *changed* you know that, Bob: "Fuck you, I don't need anyone, fuck you"...

BOBBY. And what are you, huh? You been reading "Redbook"...? What is this all of a sudden... *(pause)* You want to know how she *is?* She's *fine.*

JOEY. Well, that's all I *asked.* I ast you how she is, you *barked* at me. Fuck *you.*

BOBBY. Hey, you know, Joey, you know, people get *married...*

JOEY. Yeah. I know they do.

BOBBY. They... *(pause)*

JOEY. What? *(pause)* what? *(pause)* What? Mr. Wisdom...*speak* to me.

BOBBY. I should never have married a shiksa.

JOEY. Yeah. I know. Cause that's all that you used to say "let's find some Jew Broads and discuss the *Midrash...*"

BOBBY. This is something different.

JOEY. *Is* it?

BOBBY. Yes. I'm talking about marriage, you asked a *question,* I'm answering you. You don't want to fuckin' *talk* about it, we'll talk about something that *you* like. *(pause)*

JOEY. Tell me.

BOBBY. You know what she said?

JOEY. Who, Laurie?

BOBBY. Yeah.

JOEY. No, what.

BOBBY. Listen to this: "What are we going to tell the kids."

JOEY. She said that?

BOBBY. Yes.

JOEY. When?

BOBBY. Right before I left...

JOEY. "What are you going to tell the kids..."?

BOBBY. Yeah. *(pause)*

JOEY. What *are* you going to tell the kids?

BOBBY. What is there to tell? The kid is a Jew.

JOEY. *(pause)* Well, Bob, the law says he's a Jew, his, you know what the law says, he's a Jew his *mother* is a jew.

BOBBY. Fuck the law.

JOEY. Well, all I'm saying, that's what the law says...

BOBBY. Joey, Joey, what are you're saying, a kid of mine *isn't* going to be a Jew? What is he going to *be? Look* at him...

JOEY. I'm, I'm only talking about...

BOBBY. I know what you're talking about. What *I'm* saying, common sense? They start knocking heads in the schoolyard looking for Jews, you fuckin' think they aren't goint to take my kid because of, uh...

JOEY. No, no.

BOBBY. Well...?

JOEY. What I'm saying...

BOBBY. ...are they going to take him, or they're going to pass him up 'cause he's so...

JOEY. I'm talking about the law...

BOBBY. 'Cause he's so *blond* and all, "Let's go beat up some kikes..."

JOEY. Bobby, don't make me out the bad guy here, I only brought it up.

BOBBY. Well, listen to *this,* Joe, because I want to tell you what she *says* to me one night: "If you've been persecuted so long, eh, you must have brought it on yourself." *(pause)*

JOEY. She said that?

BOBBY. Yes. *(pause)*

JOEY. Wait a second. If we've been oppressed so long we must be doing it.

BOBBY. *(pause)* Yes.

JOEY. She said that.

BOBBY. Yes. *(pause)*

JOEY. And what did you say to her?

BOBBY. I don't know...

JOEY. What do you mean you don't know? What did you say to her?

BOBBY. Nothing. *(pause)*

JOEY. She actually said that? *(pause)*

BOBBY. And *(pause)* And I mean it got me *thinking...*

JOEY. Ho, ho, ho, ho, hold on a minute, here, ho, Bobby. Lemme tell you something. Let me tell you what she feels: she feels left *out,* Jim. Don't let that white shit get into your *head.* She feels left *out,* they got, what have they got, you talk about *community,* six drole cocksuckers at a *lawn* party somewhere: "How is your *boat...*" Fuck that shit, fuck that shit, she's got a point in my *ass,* what the fuck did *they* ever do? They can't make a *joke* for chrissake, I'll tell you something, are you sitting down, the *reason* that the goyin hate us the whole time, is *addition* they were *envious, because we wouldn't fight.* The reason we were *persecuted* because we said, hey, alright, leave me alone, those *nordic* types, alright, these *football* players, these cocksuckers in a fuckin', wrapped in *hides* come down and 'cause we don't fight back they go "Who are those people...?" *(pause)* "Hey, let's hit them in the head." Because we have our mind on higher things. *(pause)* Because we got something better to do than all day to fuckin' beat the women up and go *kill* things. My dad would puke to hear you talk that way. I swear to God. Alavasholem, he would weep with *blood,* your father, too, to hear you go that way. What are they *doing* to you out there? *Bobby. Bob*by, hey, look at me: They want to wipe it out. They *always* wanted to wipe it out. Bobby. That's why they hated Christ. And you tell me, you're on a job and you get off the plane in Birmingham they don't hate you? You're too shut off, Bob. You should come back here. *(pause)* My Dad. *(pause)* You know, when we were growing up, he always used to say: It will happen again. We used to say, huh...?

BOBBY. I remember.

JOEY. I used to say, Papa: You're *here* now. It's over. He would say, "It will happen in your lifetime." And I used to think he was a fool. But I know he was right. *(pause)* I'm sorry that now he isn't here to tell him so. *(pause)* Because I wish he was here. *(pause)*

BOBBY. V'you been out to Waldheim?

JOEY. Judy and I went last month. We try to go once a month.

BOBBY. Would you like to go out?

JOEY. We could go. Yes.

BOBBY. Just the two of us.

JOEY. I know what you're saying.

BOBBY. When can we go?

JOEY. How long will you be in town?

BOBBY. Till the weekend.

JOEY. You want to go tomorrow?

BOBBY. Yes.

JOEY. Alright. *(pause)* We'll go in the morning. *(pause)*

BOBBY. I'll pick up up.

JOEY. Alright.

BOBBY. We're really going to go.

JOEY. Alright.

SCENE THREE

JOEY. I'll tell you something *else:* I would have been a great man in Europe - I was meant to be hauling *stones,* or setting *fence*posts, something...*Look* at me: the way I'm built, and here I'm working in a fucking *rest*aurant my whole life. No wonder I'm fat. I swear to God. You know how *strong* I am? We went to Judy's folks, they had a tree had fallen in the road. Up in Wis*con*sin...?

BOBBY. Yeah...?

JOEY. I picked it up. *(pause)* They wanted me to take a *crowbar* to shove it aside the *car* could pass. I didn't know what they meant. Huh? I wasn't showing off...*you* know I'm strong...

BOBBY. ...since gradeschool.

JOEY. And Arthur says "We got to move the tree..." I picked it up, I put it over there, I put it down, he's standing there a crowbar, all their *mouths* are hung open. *(pause)* It was a big tree, too. That's what I *mean,* Bobby, that's where we should be, *farming* somewhere...*Building* things, *carrying* things...this shit is *dilute,* this is schveck this shit, I swear to God, the *doctors, teachers,* everybody, in the law, the *writers* all the time geschraiying, all those assholes, how they're lost...of course, they're lost. They should be studying *talmud*...we should be able to come to them and to say, "What is the truth...?" And they should *tell* us. What the *talmud* says, what *this* one said, What *Hillel* said, and I, I should be working on a *forge* all day. They'd say "There goes Reb Lewis, he's the strongest man in Lodz." I'd nod. "He once picked up an ox." *(pause)* Or some fucking thing. I don't know if you can pick up an ox, Bob, but I tell you, I feel in my heart I was meant to work out in the winter all day. To be *strong.* Of *course* we're schlepping all the time with heart attacks, with fat, look at this goddam *food* I sell...that stuff will *kill* you, it killed my *dad*...(This is why I say go see your grandfather...) it's food to harvest *wheat,* to *forge,* to *toil,* my father's sitting on his ass for forty years driving through *Idaho* for Gould and Gould, what did he need for nourishment...? Nothing. The women, too. He should have been...the time should come we're *sixty* we look back, our wives are there, our chi*ldr*en, the *commu*nity...and we are sitting there, we *are* something...And we've been *men!* You *know*...?

BOBBY. Yes.

JOEY. And we've *lived!* We've lived the life we were supposed to live. *(pause)* Not *this,* Bobby. Not *this*... *(pause)* I don't know, I'm getting old, I look at the snow the only thing I long that I should be in Europe.

BOBBY. I'm sure it was no picnic there.

JOEY. In Europe?

BOBBY. Yes.

JOEY. Ah, fuck, I don't *know,* Bob...I don't *know*...

BOBBY. Joe: with the Nazis...?

JOEY. *Fuck* the Nazis. Fuck the Nazis, Bob. I'm saying, give a guy a chance to stand *up*...Give 'em something to stand *for.*

BOBBY. That's very pretty, and when they stick glass rods in your dick and break them off...

JOEY. ...that was the *Japs*...

BOBBY. I'm saying, Joey, that's romantic *shit...*

JOEY. *Is* it...?

BOBBY. Because, yes, because, yes. It is. And to a certain, *yes,* it is, and to a certain extent it's, I'll tell you what it's, it's *profaning* what they went through.

JOEY. Oh. *Is* it...?

BOBBY. Yes.

JOEY. And why...

BOBBY. Because they went through it.

JOEY. They did. ...what I'm saying, that *I* could have, too, That's all I'm saying.

BOBBY. You don't know you could have...

JOEY. Yes. That's what I'm *saying,* Bob...I could...

BOBBY. ...to go through that shit in the Camps...?

JOEY. Yes.

BOBBY. No, Joe, no. You don't *know* what you would have done... *(JOEY shrugs.)* You don't know what the fuck you would have done, what you would have felt. None of us know.

JOEY. *(shrugs)* If you say so, Bob.

SCENE FOUR

JOEY. I'll tell you where I would of loved it: in The *shtetl. (pause)* I would of loved it there. You, too. You would of been Reb Gould. You would of told them what Rabbi Akiba said...

BOBBY. You think they fooled around?

JOEY. Who? In the shtetl?

BOBBY. Yeah.

JOEY. The guys in the shtetl?

BOBBY. Yeah.

JOEY. I think it was too small.

BOBBY. But when they went to town...

JOEY. When the *guys* went to town?

BOBBY. Yes.

JOEY. With Polish Whores...?

BOBBY. Yeah...

JOEY. I don't know.

BOBBY. You think you would have?

JOEY. No.

BOBBY. With some young Jewish thing...?

JOEY. *Inside* the shtetl...?

BOBBY. Yes.

JOEY. And, what, defile my home...?

BOBBY. You think you would have.

JOEY. You would be found *out...*

BOBBY. I would?

JOEY. Because you were a, *yeah.* Because you were a *Jew.* If you wanted to go out fuck around who'd have you? If you stayed home you would be found *out.* I think, *(pause)* But on the other hand who's to *say* what could go on. At night. In Europe. *(pause)* That's true, *too...(pause)* Judy would be old...she would have some incurable disease...we would be married years. But I would not be old. I would be deep in grief, and deep in contemplation of my life. Some young, the daughter of one of my customers, the orphaned daughter...is this what you're saying?

BOBBY. Yes.

JOEY. She comes to me, the whole town is silent with sympathy, "I baked this for you." *(pause)* "My father respected you so..."

BOBBY. Mmm. *(long pause)*

SCENE FIVE

JOEY. Oh, *many* times I wished to go back, to the *war,* to when my folks came here...to *Orchard* Street...you know, to *Maxwell* Street...to *push*carts...to...

BOBBY. We wouldn't have liked it.

JOEY. You think?

BOBBY. No.

JOEY. *I* don't know...

BOBBY. You know what I would, I'll tell you what I would have loved, to go, in the *twenties,* to be in *Holly*wood...

JOEY. Huh.

BOBBY. *Jesus,* I know they had a good time there. Here you got, I mean, five smart Jew boys from Russia, this whole *industry...*

JOEY. Who?

BOBBY. Who. Mayer. Warners. Fox.

JOEY. Fox? Fox is Jewish?

BOBBY. Sure.

JOEY. Fox is a Jewish name?

BOBBY. Sure.

JOEY. Who knew that?

BOBBY. Everyone.

JOEY. Huh. *(pause)* I always saw their *thing,* it looked goyish to me.

BOBBY. What thing?

JOEY. Their *castle,* that thing on their movies...

BOBBY. No.

JOEY. I thought it was a goyish name.

BOBBY. "Fox"?

JOEY. Twentieth *century* fox. *(pause) Century* fox. *(pause)* Charlie Chaplin was Jewish.

BOBBY. I know that, Joe.

JOEY. Yeah? People *fool* you. Oh, you know, you know who else was Jewish? Mr. *White...*

BOBBY. Mr. White...?

JOEY. Mr. White. On Jeffrey. The *shoe store...*? Miller-White Shoes.

BOBBY. *...yeah...?*

JOEY. On Jeffrey...?

BOBBY. He was Jewish?

JOEY. Yeah.

BOBBY. Huh.

JOEY. My mom told me.

BOBBY. He didn't look Jewish.

JOEY. That's what I'm *saying...(pause)*

BOBBY. He was a nice guy.

JOEY. Yes. He was.

BOBBY. I re*mem*ber him. They always gave you what, a lollipop somthing when you came out.

JOEY. Why do you think kids hate trying on shoes?

BOBBY. I don't *know. (pause)* You know, actually I don't

like trying them on either.

JOEY. You don't?

BOBBY. No. *(pause)*

JOEY. I don't think that I do, either. *(pause) Jimmy* does.

BOBBY. He does?

JOEY. Yeah. *(pause)* So I was reminiscing with my *mom...*

BOBBY. ...yeah...

JOEY. You know, about the *shoe* store, huh? Cause I took Jimmy into get his shoes, I'm talking about when we stopped on Pratt, I say: "The old shoestore the goyish guy, Miller's partner." So she goes "Jerry White..." He was the shamus at Temple Zion thirty years.

BOBBY. Huh.

JOEY. *Huh...?*

BOBBY. How about that. *(pause)*

JOEY. That's what I said.

BOBBY. How about that. *(pause)* He still alive?

JOEY. No. He died.

BOBBY. He died, huh?

JOEY. Yes. He did. *(pause)*

BOBBY. The store still there?

JOEY. Oh, Bobby, it's all *sch*vartz there now. *(pause) You* knew that...*(pause)*

SCENE FIVE

JOEY. Life is too short.

BOBBY. Life is very short.

JOEY. It's *very* short. We're sitting on the stoop, we're *old...(pause)* We're *married*...we have *kids*...

BOBBY. How's Judy?

JOEY. *(pause)* I *pray,* you know, I *pray,* every night I pray that I can get through life without *murdering* anybody.

BOBBY. Who would you murder?

JOEY. ...I'm saying I'm uncontrollable.

BOBBY. ...all of us are...

JOEY. ...and I got married wrong. *(pause)* well...*there, (pause)* there you are.

BOBBY. You didn't get married wrong, Joe.

JOEY. Yes. I did. You don't know. I want to tell you something, Bob, she's a wonderful woman, but there's such a thing as lust. I don't know if it's *lust.* Yes. Yes, it is: I, I, I say this is a *feeling*...I, I'm not *alone. (pause)* then I walk out the *door*...

BOBBY. We all feel like that sometimes...

JOEY. You don't know what I'm going to say, I walk out of the door I say "If I never *saw* them again, it would be fine..."

BOBBY. We all feel like that sometimes...

JOEY. Fuck you. Listen to me. I *mean* it...there are times, I'll tell you that I think a feeling gets so overpowering it becomes a *fact,* and you don't even know you did it.

Sometimes I think, "Well if they were *killed*...if they died..." and sometimes I think I'll do it myself.

BOBBY. It's just a feeling, Joe.

JOEY. I pray you'll never know it. Sometimes it goes farther. I *have* killed them, and I take the plane, I don't *call* anyone, because now I don't care; and fly to *Canada* and rent a car and go into the forest and begin to walk...I know I have to die...so I walk...and I'm going North. I feel so free. I can't tell you, Bobby...I have a pistol, I can end it any time. I feel so *free*...If I could feel like that in my *life*...I *swear* there are people who can live like that. I know there are. Who exist. Holy men. Visionaries, scholars, I *know* they exist...I know they're *cloistered*...I know that it's real. But I can't get it up. I'm going to die like this. A schmuck. I know that there is power in me. But it's not coming out. It's never coming out. The only bar between me and what I would like to do is doing it. I'll never do it, though. What do you make of that? *(long pause)*

BOBBY. You really have a gun?

JOEY. What gun?

BOBBY. You said you have a pistol...

JOEY. I said that I have a *pistol...?*

BOBBY. You said you were going North...

JOEY. In my *dream*. In my *dream*...in my *fantasy*...you know...

BOBBY. Oh. *(pause)*

JOEY. In my *imaginings...*

BOBBY. Oh. *(pause)*

JOEY. I actually *have* a pistol. In my store.

BOBBY. You do?

JOEY. Behind the counter.

BOBBY. Mm.

JOEY. For *burglars.* You worried I would shoot myself?

BOBBY. You said you would.

JOEY. I actually might. I think that sometimes. *(pause)* Don't you? *(pause)* Bobby...?

BOBBY. *(pause)* Sometimes. *(pause)*

JOEY. I knew you did. *(pause)* I wouldn't take the pistol from the store, though. And I'll tell you why, because I think that just its *presence,* that *you* know it's there discourages them. *(pause)* Let them go rob someplace else. Everything, everything, everything...it's...I'll tell you: it's a mystery... *(pause)* Everything is a mystery, Bob...*everything. (pause)* I don't know how things work. I can hang up a coathook, people that I know can fix a stove. *(pause)* Anyone can change a tire—although Lucille bought a new Pontiac, she went to change the tire, the jack wouldn't fit it.

BOBBY. Maybe she wasn't putting it in right.

JOEY. She said that she was. I think they gave her the wrong size, the custom *things* today and you can't change a fuckin' *tire* with the wrong size jack. People could *die* of something like that. Because *every*thing is so far from us today. And we have no connection...

BOBBY. There are people who have a connection.

JOEY. Who? Who are they?...and there are lives, Bobby, where people never have a thought. Where all day it is like they aren't there. Where they are a dream of their environment. I don't mean savages. Where their lives are a joy. Where questions are answered with ritual. Where life if short. We read them in the books.

BOBBY. ...what books...?

JOEY. I don't *know* what books...that's what I'm *saying*...but there are *things*...there are *things*...there...there are ways to *get* there that *exist*. They...*(pause)* In *rituals,* I'm saying that you didn't make *up,* but *existed*...they would cause you *pain*...

BOBBY. Who would?

JOEY. ...they'd take you in a hut. You'd come out, you would be a man. *(pause)* And, by God, that is what you would *be. (pause)*

BOBBY. *(pause)* I think I invent *ceremonies, but I never keep them up. I know I should, I say if I forget this now, I'll never keep it up, but I don't.*

JOEY. What? Like what?

BOBBY. Like any thing.

JOEY. Like what?

BOBBY. Like prayer.

JOEY. You don't keep up prayer?

BOBBY. No.

JOEY. What? Did you used to pray?

BOBBY. I've prayed.

JOEY. Judy and I joined a synagogue.

BOBBY. You did?

JOEY. Yeah.

BOBBY. Which one?

JOEY. It's new.

BOBBY. Up by you?

JOEY. Yeah. *(pause)*

BOBBY. What do you do, you *go* there...

JOEY. ...we just joined...

BOBBY. You *did.*

JOEY. Yeah. *(pause)*

BOBBY. Hey you *know?*

JOEY. Yeah, I know.

BOBBY. What?

JOEY. I *know.*

BOBBY. *(sigh)* Joey...Joey...Joey.

JOEY. Bushes are steel.

BOBBY. Bushes are steel. Yes, they are. Yes, they are. God *damn* me. *(pause)* D'you ever think that we would live to be this old?

JOEY. No. *(pause)* I never thought about it. *(pause)*

BOBBY. You think we're getting old?

JOEY. Yeah. *(pause)* I suppose we are. *(pause)* Isn't everybody?

SCENE SIX

BOBBY. You remember the Sleepy Time Motel?

JOEY. Yes.

BOBBY. Is it still there?

JOEY. Yes, it is.

BOBBY. You remember when Elizabeth Carpenter threw up?

JOEY. Yes.

BOBBY. Those girls. *(pause)*

JOEY. Yeah. I remember...

BOBBY. *(pause) Eliz*beth...*Deeny.*

JOEY. Deeny. I see her now and then. She works at Fields.

BOBBY. She does?

JOEY. She got divorced.

BOBBY. I didn't even know that she was married.

JOEY. She got married million years ago.

BOBBY. When did she get divorced?

JOEY. Not too long, maybe a year ago. Two years.

BOBBY. And how is she?

JOEY. Yeah. She's fine.

BOBBY. Did she get fat?

JOEY. No. *(pause)* She's selling cosmetics on the first floor.

BOBBY. She is?

JOEY. Yeah.

BOBBY. She ever ask about me?

JOEY. Yeah.

BOBBY. What does she say?

JOEY. How were you.

BOBBY. What did you tell her?

JOEY. That you're fine. *(pause)*

BOBBY. She works at the place downtown or on Michigan?

JOEY. Michigan.

BOBBY. Cosmetics.

JOEY. Yeah.

BOBBY. What does she look like?

JOEY. She looks the same.

BOBBY. She does?

JOEY. Yeah. I'm *struck* by that sometimes. I mean *you* look the same to me.

BOBBY. Isn't that funny, cause you look the same to me.

JOEY. You think that's funny?

BOBBY. Yeah.

JOEY. I think it's funny, too. I wish I had a cigarette.

BOBBY. Yes. I do, too. *(pause)*

JOEY. You wanna go get some?

BOBBY. I almost do, but I shouldn't.

JOEY. No. I shouldn't either. *(pause)* Isn't that something?

BOBBY. Yes. It is.

GOLDBERG STREET

GOLDBERG STREET was first presented live on WNUR Radio in Chicago on March 4, 1985, with the following cast directed by David Mamet:

MAN .... Mike Nussbaum

DAUGHTER........................ Susan Nussbaum

GOLDBERG STREET

A man and his daughter talking.

MAN. Goldberg Street. Because they didn't *have* it.
They had *Smith* Street—they had *Rybka* Street.
There was no Goldberg Street.
You can keep your distance and it's fine.
If a man is secluded then he feels superior. Or rage. But where's the good in that?

DAUGHTER. There is no good in it.

MAN. I'm not sure. And I'm not so sure. But sometimes... *(pause)* And sometimes, also—you must stand up for yourself. Because it is uncertain...what we're doing here. And masses of *people* do now this and now that; and *at the moment* you might say "this seems wrong," or "this seems attractive." Popular delusions warp...you cannot say they are the product of one man.
Some men like hunting. I enjoy it myself.
Some men like to kill.
Many have killed. Many would say this is not a bad thing.
But they know it is.
Which is not to say they have not enjoyed it.

. . . . .

MAN. A man would *wish...(pause)* A man would wish someone to inform him...I, if A man, say, this is a good example—I am not mechanical but if something is broken and I *must* fix it there comes a point at which pride *in myself*—for the alternative is to say that I am not a man, or that I am an impotent or *stupid*...or, in some way unable to do those things many have done...At one point I would say: "It now is mine to fix it." When it's up to *me*—if there is no one there...then I *will* fix it—for it isn't hidden. So with problems...those things where one *cannot* refer to someone. At some point. One must say: *I* am the...

DAUGHTER. ...the authority.

MAN. ...the, *lonliness* that that entails, of course...and who would be so droll as to form a religion on ethical principles? *(pause)*
And one is alone.
And so one is...
And so what.
From *that* one may say "well, then I can proceed..."
Lost in the wood you must say "I am lost."

DAUGHTER. You killed the deer.

MAN. The man in *Bregny...(pause)* Men hunted them with automatic weapons. Which is not a sporting way and it is not an effective way. Because you can't *aim* them, truly...

DAUGHTER. ...because they jump.

MAN. They *do* jump. And...you can aim the first shot, of course... But we were taught to fire them from the hip. Held on the sling to give it tension. And they *hunted* them, and, as you couldn't aim your shot, the animal, hit badly...
Ran.

Died.
Left a blood trail, but they couldn't follow it.
Or wouldn't.
Although they were country boys.
And, I'm sure...revered life.
Loved hunting...
...anyway
(pause)
They couldn't read a compass.
In Arkansas one time we were lost. The leader asked if anyone could read a compass. We'd all heard the lecture. I said, well, I'd never *held* one, but I heard it, I supposed I...took it. Read it. Followed the map. Led us back to camp. It was easy enough. None of it was difficult. And they put me in for the Unit. When they asked for volunteers. Which may have been a joke. It was a joke. For anti-Semitism in the army. Then. Even now...*(pause)* Even for, and especially then which I see as...If you look at the world you have to laugh. They scorned me, as I assume they did, for those skills they desired to possess. And it was funny I had them. To them. Lost in the woods. It seems simple enough. If you just take away the thought of someone's coming to help you. *(pause)*

DAUGHTER. You never see them?

MAN. No, although we were close. In a way. Over there. Where would we...I have no desire to go down south. *(pause)* To go visiting at all.

DAUGHTER. You went to France.

MAN. I did. It was the Anniversary. I wanted to see.

DAUGHTER. What did you see? *(pause)*

MAN. People. *(pause)* I saw the town.

DAUGHTER. Had it changed?

MAN. No. It hadn't changed. Just as the world has changed. *(pause)*

DAUGHTER. I heard they saw you.

MAN. Yes. They saw me. There's always someone there. Laying flowers—its right by the cliff. I mean the cliff is right beside the road. They...*(pause)*

DAUGHTER. They knew you.

MAN. I was...no, they didn't know me. They saw someone standing...*(pause)*A man spoke English. He went in the pub. He must have said, he said something like "one of them's come back." And, in the cemetery...they came over there.

DAUGHTER. You were reading the stones?

MAN. They're crosses, really...*(pause)* Yes. I was looking for the names.

DAUGHTER. Did you find them?

MAN. I thought that I would not remember them. I...but I...*(pause)* People from the pub came out. *(pause)* They said, "You were here."
Yes. We wept.
Patton slapped that Jewish boy.
They said...*(pause)*

DAUGHTER. They remembered you. *(pause)* They remembered what you'd done.

MAN. They sent me for a joke. Because I read the compass. I was glad to go. I knew they thought me ludicrous. Our shame is that we feel they're right. *(pause)* I...have no desire to go to Israel. *(pause)* But I went to France.

THE LUFTMENSCH

CHARACTERS

Two older men, A & B

THE LUFTMENSCH

SCENE ONE

Two older men.

A. Well, he, what he found, they weren't the same.

B. Some of them were.

A. None of them were. That's what he — old days, he would, Polack moldmakers...

B. ...what did they...?

A. ...the South Side, I don't know. There was an area of...

B. ...Hegewisch.

A. ...Alphabetville, all those, down by Gary. Polack, you...

B. Bohemians.

A. Exactly. All of them gone. Uk...Ukraina...Boznia, Herz...all of, what did I? All gypsies to me—

B. ...to all of us.

A. All those *tinkers*—I don't know if I remembered it or

B. ...read it...

A. ...or of I did. I *think* horses—in the street. Swarthy...those, of course, would be different.

B. The workers would.

A. Yes. What I'm—men. Heads like a block of wood. He'd...Men...

B. You don't see them anymore.

A. I'm saying that you don't...

B. In comm...

A. Not even th...

B. ...in Communist Countries. In Pictures.

A. Not even there. What they lack...

B. ...a look of freed...

A. What they lack, ten, fifteen hundred years of... some...some mystic...freed here, in their final moments, who would say...

B. He'd?

A. No. I *thought* it—he would not say. What He'd: "Made a Sale!"

B. To?

A. In the *steelmills*—come home—because he'd *drink* with them. You know?

B. In the mills...

A. In the taverns by them.

B. And the men accept...?

A. They *loved* him.

B. *(simultaneous with "loved")* They accepted him?

A. They *loved* him. Listen: he: you see, the admiration that he had, "Some sonofabitch, eighty years old, walked the ridgepole. Climbed..." Or, "In the mills, I swear to Christ, a man could not stand *straight,* and, let alone *work,* the heat they..." Fifty years *later*—laws, regulations...for the...*(pause)* For the...*(Pause. Sighs. Long pause.)* For. The. Safety. of. the. workers. there. *(pause)* No, but not them. *(pause)* Men who drank for breakfast. *(pause)* One time, he was out on the prairies. Harvest time. Thirty-two men, sat to lunch. Each one a loaf of bread, the women, too.

Still, in his heart...

B. ...the Mills.

A. Yes. They were his people. Talked to him. Played music, that's the...Yes, you see? They knew he was a Jew. I, I, you know, they say "Jude Suss," our Good...

B. ...the tame boy.

A. ...our little, not him. This was, any day he chose to turn his hand, he walked down there, he sold them. Eighty ninety dollars. In commission. To *himself.*

B. ...this is in Thirty-...?

A. I don't know. It doesn't make a difference. How? He *loved* those men. *(pause)* He *loved* those men. They loved *him.* You see: *(pause)* What they, it was not the Language of *Exiles*—it...*(pause)* He spoke to all of them, of course. He spoke all of their...they, you know. See: this is the sad thing. Languages they spoke. They're gone. The States are gone. They never were written. The dialects. You see. People refer to them in books. He *spoke* them. European...he spoke *Gypsy.* What is that? Egyptian...He spoke all their languages. He was a bird. He never *thought to turn his hand to any of it. Any of the work.*

B. ...the work he loved...

A. He had no guilt. He had no remorse. He had nothing. He would *spend* the fees and we had no food. *(pause)* Later. In...*far (pause) Far* north. "Rosemead." some... "Rose"..."Rose"...something...

B. Rosemont.

A. No. *(pause) Glenrose (pause)* glen...*(pause)* Isn't that funny? *(pause)* I used to go there to...

B. ...see him.

A. ...to see him. Yes. *Far*...by the Fox *River*...*(pause) Far* away. It's all part of some, now...No. It's farther than that. Far...may...you know, that *current*—European...love of. *Outdoors*...Rolling, and you might say, "Mystical"...for who would come here to be slaves to buildings? Sometimes I dream. I wonder if it is still, I know that it is gone, but sometimes I dream that one pocket of it still exists...you wouldn't meet a boy under a tree. *(pause)* A boy fishing. *(pause)* A...a...*(pause)* A bandstand. *(pause)* Or hunting squirrels, or...

B. You went to see him there.

A. ...or, someone told me once. sleighbells—the young men would go courting and pack *snow,* so as not to wake the girl's parents. *(pause)* As the horse went along. *(pause)* At the end of day a man, a *fit* man, who worked hard, sometimes he'd want to fight. *Want* to drink...want run, run, go, run around, find a woman, *fuck* her. Want...some, they had crimes, of course, down by the River; by the Lake. They say—perhaps they do *not* say, but I know—that crime seeks out the low places—madmen in the quarries—saints on mountain tops—those men in the mills sweating out their lives. Yes. It was *right. Yes.* Bronzed. Drink a pint of rum for breakfast. *Whiskey...*

B. ...some countries they start the day with wine.

A. *(simultaneous with "start") This* is the foreign land, he would not have said, but I say.

SCENE TWO

A. Things that he had locked in there.

B. What were they?

A. I...a coin collection. *(pause)* I *think.*

B. You don't re...?

A. I'm not...*yes.* I can, how can I say I'm...if you *opened* it...

B. ...if it were opened.

A. You would say: if you opened it and it was not there you'd, "Yes, he was sure, but he was *mistaken*"

B. Are you?

A. *(simultaneous with "you")* As I very well may be. *Yes.* You would say "certainty"—but what is it? Obstinence.

B. ...religious...

A. Even that.—Whatever you say. What is it? It's nothing. He put policies in there. Gold? He had no. I saw a movie and presumed there was an old revolver. But there was not. Coins, I somehow...old.

B. Foreign?

A. I don't...

B. Valuable?

A. How can I? Nothing he touched was. You might say, "the small silver..." (whatever) the irony is, after all that time "they had a fortune at their feet." And what would it mean now? The irony was *fate,* if you will... he...that every thing was of a piece. There *was* no valuable coin—there *was* no illuminating letter there—and what would it illuminate? It was locked and he'd lost the key—someone had lost it. They said for a while—family (what would you say?) *history.* A "Joke." It was "held," is the way to say it—that *I* had.

B. Was that true?

A. No.

B. What was true?

A. That it was a safe. That it was locked. That there was nothing valuable in it.

SCENE THREE

A. In his house there was a white picket fence. He kept an animal a goat I'm sure it was. For Milk? For? *(pause)* For tradition—and, you see that this old man—so tied to the ways of his youth. Became a Friendly Woodcutter. Never did a day's work in his life. Died poor. Died happy. On the one hand his friends were the very people who had over the course of a thousand years destroyed his race—could you say they were reunited here? In what? The Sun of a brighter Day? A Fresh Start? Fifty short years before it was over once again. Ash on his vest. Cigar Ash. Papers in his lapel pocket. You've seen men like that. Bound in a rubberband. He left his family. He could not understand Men on the Plains. But brought brought—finally what was that culture but the love of Death?—in Greek you say "philosophy." In Gypsies, in Teutonic, in the Northern Races, what? All of them drank. I drink. Everyone drinks. No one today works. That last vestige of Europe. On the Far South Side. He loved the Polish. Who at Home...but in a Foreign Soil...Moved West. The intermediate land of the Lotos Eaters. Fed on Pine. A Funny Spirit of the Indians. He found it all a transient joke, or, but, you see, you must *embrace* it. He found it was his to choose, over so quickly, died so young. What did he leave us? For it all was sold. Except he smiled. Except he talked with them in pubs. We didn't care that he did not come home. Then but not now. I wish that I had gone with him.

Other Publications for Your Interest

LAKEBOAT

(ADVANCED GROUPS—COMEDY)

By DAVID MAMET

8 men—Unit set

This fascinating series of vignettes, staged to great acclaim by the Milwaukee Repertory Theatre, is set aboard a Great Lakes steamer, bound from Gary to Duluth. It focuses in on the eight-member crew, the hardhats of the steel waterways, all but one of whom are "lifers." The other character is a young college man who has been hired to replace the night cook. He is the closest thing to the central figure. ". . . the show has much of Mamet's poetry of the inarticulate, the ritual, tribal double-talk that makes sense underneath the ludicrous patters of our lives."—Chicago Tribune. ". . . a banquet of meaty acting parts."—Milwaukee Sentinel. (#14017)

(Slightly Restricted. Royalty, $50-$35.)

GLENGARRY GLEN ROSS

(ADVANCED GROUPS—COMIC DRAMA)

By DAVID MAMET

7 men—2 Interiors

Winner of the London theatre equivalent of our Tony Award, this scalding comedy went on to take Broadway by storm, winning the Pulitzer Prize for dramá in 1984. Never has Mr. Mamet's ear for the rhythms of actual, contemporary speech been more keen than in this tale of cutthroat real estate salesmen competing against each other for the money of unwary customers. One suavely vicious salesman, Richard Roma, is in the lead for the monthly sales award: a new Cadillac. Another, Shelly "The Machine" Levene, a former top salesman, is now riding a streak of bad luck on a smile and a shoeshine, hoping to turn his luck around. All are dependent upon an office manager named Williamson to give them the vital "leads" to new customers. Williamson, meanwhile, is pitting them against each other to drive up sales. In the first act, composed of three scenes, we meet the salesmen, vying for position as they gulp their cocktails in the local Chinese restaurant. The second act becomes a sort of "who done it" as the scene shifts to the office, where a burglary has taken place. The vital leads have been filched the night before, possibly by one of the salesmen. In the end, Williamson screws Roma out of his car and nabs the bag man. "Crackling tension . . . ferocious comedy and drama. A top American playwright in bristling form."—N.Y. Times. "Wonderfully funny . . . a play to see, remember and cherish."—N.Y. Post. "Mamet is . . . a pure writer, and the synthesis he appears to be making, with echoes from voices as diverse as Beckett, Pinter and Hemingway, is unique and exciting."—Newsweek. (#9058)

**(Restricted New York City and 100 mile radius.
Also restricted metropolitan Los Angeles, Philadelphia and New Haven.
Royalty, $60-$40.)**

Other Publications for Your Interest

THE SQUARE ROOT OF LOVE

(ALL GROUPS—FOUR COMEDIES)

By DANIEL MELTZER

1 man, 1 woman—4 Simple Interiors

This full-length evening portrays four preludes to love—from youth to old age, from innocence to maturity. Best when played by a single actor and actress. **The Square Root of Love.** Two genius-level college students discover that Man (or Woman) does not live by intellectual pursuits alone . . . **A Good Time for a Change.** Our couple are now a successful executive and her handsome young male secretary. He has decided it's time for a change, and so has she . . . **The Battling Brinkmires.** George and Marsha Brinkmire, a middle-aged couple, have come to Haiti to get a "quickie" divorce. This one has a surprise ending . . . **Waiting For To Go.** We are on a jet waiting to take off for Florida. He's a retired plumbing contractor who thinks his life is over—she's a recent widow returning to her home in Hallandale. The play, and the evening, ends with a beginning . . . A success at off-off Broadway's Hunter Playwrights. Requires only minimal settings. (#21314)

SNOW LEOPARDS

(LITTLE THEATRE—COMIC DRAMA)

By MARTIN JONES

2 women—Exterior

This haunting little gem of a play was a recent crowd-pleaser Off Off Broadway in New York City, produced by the fine StageArts Theatre Co. Set in Lincoln Park Zoo in Chicago in front of the snow leopards' pen, the play tells the story of two sisters from rural West Virginia. When we first meet Sally, she has run away from home to find her big sister Claire June, whose life Up North she has imagined to be filled with all the promise and hopes so lacking Down Home. Turns out, life in the Big City ain't all Sally and C.J. thought it would be: but Sally is going to stay anyway, and try to make her way. "Affecting and carefully crafted . . . a moving piece of work."—New York City Tribune. *Actresses take note*: this play is a treasure trove of scene and monologue material. *Producers take note*: the play may be staged simply and inexpensively. (#21245)

Other Publications for Your Interest

ADVICE TO THE PLAYERS

(DRAMA)

By BRUCE BONAFEDE

5 men, 1 woman (interracial)—Interior

Seldom has a one-act play created such a sensation as did *Advice to the Players* at Actors Theatre of Louisville's famed Humana Festival of New American Plays. Mr. Bonafede has crafted an ingenious play about two Black South African actors, here in America to perform their internationally-acclaimed production of *Waiting for Godot.* The victims of persecution in their own country, here in the U.S. they become the victims of a different kind of persecution. The anti-apartheid movement wants a strong political gesture—they want the performance cancelled. And, they are willing to go to any lengths to achieve this aim—including threatening the families of the actors back home. Cleverly, Mr. Bonafede juxtaposes the predicament of Didi and Gogo in *Waiting for Godot* with the predicament of the two actors. Both, in an odd, ironic way, are Theatre of the Absurd. "A short play blazing with emotional force and moral complexities . . . taut, searing inquiry into the inequities frequently perpetrated in the name of political justice . . . a stunning moment of theatrical truth."—Louisville Courier-Journal. (#3027)

APPROACHING LAVENDAR

(COMIC DRAMA)

By JULIE BECKETT CRUTCHER

3 women—Interior

While their father is marrying his fourth wife sardonic, controlled Jenny and her slightly neurotic housewife-sister Abigail wait in a church vestibule. There they encounter Wren, the spacey ingenue who is about to become their step-sister. The mood of polite tolerance degenerates with comic results as inherent tensions mount and the womens' conflicted feelings about their parents' remarriage surface. The contingent self-discovery results in new understanding and forgiveness, and ultimately reveals the significance of sisterhood. Highly-praised in its debut at the famed Actors Theatre of Louisville, the play was singled out by the Louisville press for its "precise and disquieting vision" as well as its sharp humor, as it "held a capacity audience rapt." (#3649)

A TANTALIZING

(DRAMA)

By WILLIAM MASTROSIMONE

1 man, 1 woman—Interior

Originally produced by the amazing Actors Theatre of Louisville, this is a new one-act drama by the author of *The Woolgatherer* and *Extremities. A Tantalizing* is about the attempts by a young woman to "save" a street bum, a tattered and crazy old man whom she has dragged in off the street. Like Rose in *Extremities* she, too, has secrets in her closet. What these secrets are is the intriguing mystery in the plot of the play, as we gradually realize why the woman has taken such an interest in the bum. (#22021)

Other Publications for Your Interest

SEASCAPE WITH SHARKS AND DANCER

(LITTLE THEATRE—DRAMA)

By DON NIGRO

1 man, 1 woman—Interior

This is a fine new play by an author of great talent and promise. We are very glad to be introducing Mr. Nigro's work to a wide audience with *Seascape With Sharks and Dancer*, which comes directly from a sold-out, critically acclaimed production at the world-famous Oregon Shakespeare Festival. The play is set in a beach bungalow. The young man who lives there has pulled a lost young woman from the ocean. Soon, she finds herself trapped in his life and torn between her need to come to rest somewhere and her certainty that all human relationships turn eventually into nightmares. The struggle between his tolerant and gently ironic approach to life and her strategy of suspicion and attack becomes a kind of war about love and creation which neither can afford to lose. In other words, this is quite an offbeat, wonderful love story. We would like to point out that the play also contains a wealth of excellent *monologue* and *scene material.* (#21060)

GOD'S SPIES

(COMEDY)

By DON NIGRO

1 man, 2 women—Interior

This is a truly hilarious send-up of "Christian" television programming by a talented new playwright of wit and imagination. We are "on the air" with one of those talk shows where people are interviewed about their religious conversions, offering testimonials of their faith up to God and the Moral Majority. The first person interview by stalwart Dale Clabby is Calvin Stringer, who discourses on devil worship in popular music. Next comes young Wendy Trumpy, who claims to have talked to God in a belfry. Her testimonial, though, is hardly what Dale expected . . . Published with *Crossing the Bar*. (#9643)

CROSSING THE BAR

(COMEDY)

By DON NIGRO

1 man, 2 women—Interior

Two women sit in a funeral parlor with the corpse of a recently-deceased loved one, saying things like "Doesn't he look like himself", when the corpse sits up, asking for someone named Betty. Who is this Betty, they wonder? God certainly works in mysterious ways . . . Published with *God's Spies*. (#5935)

Other Publications for Your Interest

MOVIE OF THE MONTH

(COMEDY)

By DANIEL MELTZER

2 men—Interior

This new comedy by the author of the ever-popular *The Square Root of Love* is an amusing satire of commercial television. B.S., a TV programming executive, is anxious to bolster his network's ratings, which have been sagging of late due to programming disasters such as a documentary called "The Ugly Truth" (says B.S.: "What the hell is The Ugly Truth, and how the hell did it get into our Prime Time?") His eagerbeaver assistant, appropriately named Broun, has found a script which he is sure can be made into a hit "Movie of the Month". It's about this Danish prince, see, who comes home from college to find that his uncle has murdered his father and married his mother . . . Well, naturally, B.S. has his own ideas about how to fix such a totally unbelievable plot . . . (#17621)

SUNDANCE

(ALL GROUPS—COMEDY)

By MEIR Z. RIBALOW

5 men—Simple interior

This new comedy from the author of *Shrunken Heads* is set in a sort of metaphysical wild west saloon. The characters include Hickock, Jesse, the Kid, and the inevitable Barkeep. Hickock kills to uphold the law. Jesse kills for pleasure. The Kid kills to bring down The Establishment. What if, wonders the Barkeep, they met up with the Ultimate Killer—who kills for no reason, who kills simply because that's what he does? Enter Sundance. He does not kill to uphold the law, for pleasure, or to make a political statement, or because he had a deprived childhood. And he proceeds to kill everyone, exiting at the end with his sixguns blazing! "Witty, strong, precise, unusually well-written."—The Guardian. "A brilliant piece."—Dublin Evening Press. This co-winner of the 1981 Annual NYC Metropolitan Short Play Festival has been a success in 6 countries! (#3113)